FROM SOMEONE WHO PERCEIVES THROUGH FLY EYES

(Collection of poems)

SK Iyer

ISBN: 9781977053961

©

Preface

Fly eyes have the fastest visual responses in the animal kingdom. Thousands of ommatidia generate thousands of sights, thousands of thoughts and thousands of tiny images - an almost 360-degree view of the world around it. Nothing is in order. Nothing is in focus (or all are in focus?). The mind views it all at random and generates silly to serious to funny images.

'From someone who perceives through fly eyes' is a collection of poems, including a long one. Through simple words, the poet gives a deep thought over small things, which are usually overlooked or ignored. Some of the poems are witty and make the reader laugh and at the same time to think.

TABLE OF CONTENTS

7

In loving memory of my Usha

the spects on the table
look at me
without her eyes

ABOUT THE AUTHOR

SK Iyer, a commerce graduate with a flair for writing, is presently leading a retired but busy life in Pune, India. He started associating with an English daily, though on a small scale, writing articles during 1990-95. During his seven-year stint in Dubai (1995-2002), his attention turned to poetry, which he has been nurturing as a hobby. Several of his poems have been published in print and on the Internet, mostly in the USA and UK. He is a member of PK Poetry List, UK.

Mind seeks the way of perception
To reach unknown destination
No compass, but faith shows direction

WHAT IS THE GREATEST EXTRAVAGANCE?

Spending time on writing
continuous sentences
without a pause
beyond the end of a line
couplet or stanza
and calling it a
p
o
e
m
extravagance
of enjambements

ABSTRACT ABSURDITIES

broken   castle   of   life

jumpy

heart   beats

blast

empty

splinters   hurt

to   the   tune   of

abstract   absurdities

SUPPOSITITIOUS HYPOTHESIS

waves gather all the silver pearls from the sun
head toward the rocky shore to break and scatter
their determination and merge into the sea
of nothingness

DEMOCRATIC AUTOCRACY

is it another civic charm revealing
a vagrant vision of a democratic impression
or embodiment of power of the people
a dramatised truth touches me
in the theater of democracy a taste of comedy

he who was in power is a vestige now
the sacrifice is over.
several of him of the same blood raise
to share the freedom freed from him
representing the people
in the name of democracy
plural form of autocracy

now the altar is again set
by the people for the people

ENVIOUS SELF

Feelings are many,
many are useless,
like munching peanuts sitting on a beach,
to pass the time and count the waves.

Waves -
they walk back and forth,
as the crabs ashore imitate,
from present to future
and back to the past.
Envious self could only look back…

A BELIEVER'S ATHEISM

the doctrines of belief and non-belief
flaunt the uber-luxury of faith.
either way god lives in everyone -
an atheist will always remember him
that there is no he and the others
will have the option of agnosticism

for john the drunkard of our village
life's in a few pints
every time he passes the church
would pray for money for his next dose

once he prayed   god gimme ten bucks
and i will offer half of it to you
promptly he found five bucks on the road
and he didn't forget to thank god:
god you're very honest and wise
retained your share and paid me five bucks

FAILING WORDS

bright impressions are swallowed by shadows
of lumpy patches of words; rhythm jerks
forward in a world where everything
is strangely familiar like this evening
which paints its own portrait on the horizon
every day - a new face, new concepts, in new hues

and the poet fails as usual; yet he tries
to pick up scattered pieces of truth
from the bank of memory, blot the ripples
in the dust of silence and look for words
in the black sky touching the other side of the lake -
the words, which can change colours every day, like
evenings

SIN LADEN BIN

wake up the sleeping window
eyes escape through the grill
the golden round rises above
the poultry shop across the empty road
a cockerel breaks the dawn

a sudden twist
sun sets at dawn
the head is severed
a few headless flaps
an exploding silence
the link to this world goes off

windows to the world shut
as if nothing has happened

BEREAVED KNIFE

"Please allow me to kill you",
implored the honest butcher,
and sprinkled a little water
on the face of the animal.
It shook its head
as if in agreement,
and the knife went down.
Butcher relieved a sinless sigh,
bereaved knife shed tears,

in red.

HOW MANY TIMES THE WORLD IS KILLED?

the goats tied to the lamppost across
the road, opposite the butcher's shop,
chew down their hunger for fig leaves

one by one will see soon the death of
the entire world right before their eyes

DISTANT HORIZON

As nature gave my hair a colour of peace;
I yearned for peace of mind.
Mind, the mother of thoughts,
tinged with myriad colours of thoughts,
weakened by friction of time,
longed for a peaceful evening of life.
I sat on the rock, with gloomy eyes,
as evening zephyr murmured in my ears:
"I am time, the eternal, the deathless,
mentor of your destiny.
Life's a day's work from dawn to dusk,
yearn to live it in the shine of bask.
Striving to enjoy my eternity;
you, fool, you are bereft,
of the moonlit night, which's a myth,
as the evening of life entombs you.
Don't swagger, you may see your second childhood,
for, your destiny is in my hand.
Behind the cerulean sky,
where your eyes have no wings to reach,
flies your greedy mind with imaginary wings,
to ascend the throne of life after death."
Yet, when the night devoured the Sun,
I stood at the noon of my life.

I was triumphant, as the evening died,
to welcome the cool moonlit night,
moon-struck, on a new moon night!

As the breeze flowed into my ears,
Time said: "The sunset you see,
is not the sunset of your life.
Morrows are the soothsayers of sorrows,
sorrows are the dead of yesterdays;
barrows on the tombs of yesterdays,
are hallowed by those of yesterdays,
and followed by those of today,
and in the shadows will follow unknown morrows."
Bellowed my harrowing mind in disgust,
as time continued in my ears,
"Swallow the fear of death,
follow the reality, the eternal truth."
Yet slough of despond preyed on my mind,
mournful evening bid farewell to the day;
wail of woe sang the song of death,
as I stood at the noon of my life,
in the tranquility of the dead evening.

THROUGH THE FRAMES OF VISUAL ART

i walk, a load of sun on my head,
feeding on thoughts ideas go wilder -
sign of visual assumptions

spider weaves but not to cover
its nudity, candles carry flames
only to feed hungry darkness

branches of a dead tree draw
black lightening in the blue sky
not even a leaf moves in windstorm

tidal waves sweep my doorstep
the mountain of innovation
bathes in a tsunami of concepts

A GIFT IS A GIFT

A gift is a gift yet it would find its way
to the attic one day, for the showcase is
too small, and the love would be kept away
in the storehouse of cherished memories.
But the small silver case of Majumder was
the most blessed gift ever I came across;
sniffing a pinch of snuff from the silver case,
he would introduce to his guests always:
"This was gifted by my friend James",
his face filled with an imposing brightness.
Those who knew Majumder would know James,
who remains an unknown friend of his times.
Now the small silver box is in the showcase,
reminding a friendship that time could not erase.

A Moment of Coolness

Celsius crosses forty,
air stops its movement,
I feel thirsty,
open the tap,
air blows out....

A moment of coolness!

BELIEF

My conceptions are at the crossroads of ignorance!
Beliefs, based on baseless foundations,
like writing on the face of water,
do not believe in deliverance.

Ideas clash, thoughts scatter,
and from every splinter rise individual contentions;
pushing and pulling, from all directions,
life is caught in the whirlpool of beliefs (or
ignorance?).

BLIND VISION

He can see with his lost eyes:
dancers of his boyhood,
animals in the zoo,
curves of a woman,
wrinkles of depression,
colours of day and night....

He now sees all through his fingers,
with a piece of soft wax in his hands,
puts in place the pieces within him:

a woman of Rajasthan with
a pot of water on her head -

a product of blind vision
shows no detail, no colour,
but life and feeling.

CARVERS' MARKS?

Let this be a tribute
to those unknown unfortunates,
who carved out from hard rock
many temples,
many statues,
many deities;
and were pushed into anonymity
by the kings who found
happiness in arrogance.

Architectural competitions
among kings, the visible gods,
and in the race
many talented artisans
lost their hands
lost their eyes
lost their lives
like the sculptor of Ugrachandadevi*
to save the marvels as
the only masterpieces in the world

*King Bhupatindra Malla was greatly impressed by the sculpture of
Ugracandadevi (1707) and he had the right hand of the sculptor cut off. Many
such instances can be traced out from the history of mankind.

CHASE

Chase, chase and chase,
the dog moved with ease,
sniffing the felonious scent,
hours churned out miles of chase.

Tired of the trial, the men were bound
to trail behind the trained hound.
Everything starts has to stop,
the chase ended at a bus stop.

The weary squad concluded,
the thief had escaped,
leaving no trail behind,
and the mission came to an end.

Had the scent lost its smell
or was the dog wise enough to fool
the men at the abandoned bus stop,
where no buses would stop?

CHILDHOOD

I was in the chair, thinking,
when she came in, smiling,
an angel without wings,
and got into my bed.
Saw in her smile,
the lure of innocent love;
her charming face
drew me toward her.
Lied by her side,
she cuddled up
cozily against my chest.
Felt her warm body,
softer than butter;
Kissed her eyes
and then her cheeks;
felt the sweet smell
of the pure childhood -
the life's magnificent chapter
that seeks refuge in oblivion
never to be read by oneself.

CLONE?

She dwells the pavement -
queen of destitution.
Lusty eyes pierce her peeping flesh
miserly ones close their eyes
kindly ones drop a few coins.

She now walks past me,
clad in red and dark brown
kameez with churidar,
pushing a trolley full of grocery....!

Is it she?

CREATION

Glancing through lexicon, looking for words,
counting syllables, making notes, I spend
my evening hours amid reference books.
Thoughts were many, but refused to blend
into a palette full of shades and colours.
Through the window I saw an impatient
man hanging around in the corridors
of the maternity ward; an ardent
pain of love enclosed his face in tenseness,
activating a calmness of suspense.
The new arrival would soon fill his ears
with crying moments of happiness.
Another stage, another set, one more scene,
a new creation there but here there's nothing to be
seen.

CURTAIN

Why is there a curtain to cover up?

Without the curtain people know,
with the curtain people know more.

DARKENED BELIEF

He sat on the stairway to the temple,
head in his palms, elbows on knees.
Crowd moved in, minds soaked in faith,
with oblations and prayers,
and came out with gratification.
He saw all, but none minded him.
He cried out: "I am god",
he was told, "You are mad".
Disappointed, he disappeared
into the darkness of belief.

DAYBREAK

sleep enters my
eyes, in the darkness
another darkness

sweet darkness
in the coffee cup
day breaks

in the garden
petals burst from buds
day breaks

butterflies arrive
noiseless undulations
a new departure

DEAR LIFE...

Dear Life,
Did you say you were my friend?
I know the depth of your friendship,
like a shadow that lives only in light,
you know only to follow me.
Did you say you were leading me?
But where to? Toward destruction?
You are the coward I have ever seen,
at the sight of death you run away,
in search of another shelter!
Did I address you 'dear' Life?
You are no longer dear to me,
you are more hateful than the monster death.
Yet when the doomsday dawns,
the light in my eyes say goodbye,
I will cry for you, my Life,
for my friendship is so…….. deeper than yours!

DIET WALK

Put on kilos as some age, while
some gain due to their lifestyle.
My love for food brings tongue full of taste;
as belly bulges out in distaste.
A few speedy steps and I gasp,
lungs fail to hold air in its grasp.
In the flood of people, the pavement sinks;
civilisation in the gutter stinks.
The lady in front is double in size,
it seems, her diet walks on the bad side;
to walk behind her is doubly wise,
to keep the sun on the other side.
As the crowd moves at snail's pace
my sightless feet look for some space.

DISTRESS AND RELIEF

On the floating leaf
the ant was surveying
the boundaries of its life
restricted by a watery grave.
The tiny life was desperate
to regain its lost freedom.
Life needs the whole world;
death is content with a grave!
The river flowed lazily,
the leaf drifted slowly,
the ant moved uneasily,
my mind turned saintly.
Gently I lifted the leaf,
placed it on the bank,
the ant stepped out meekly,
idled for a little while,
moving its antennae up and down,
as if saying something to me
and disappeared among the grass;
a sigh of relief I sent out.
Did it say goodbye to me?
Or showered its blessings on me?
Silent screams of the distressed life,
still resound in my ears.

EXPECTATION

My word, like a stone thrown into a well,
settles down in some corner of your mind
or like raindrops on a lotus leaf,
roll off leaving behind no trace?

I send another word, from my mind -
imagine, not my image, but my mind
wrapped in intonations of pure love;
and here I wait for you to respond.

FANATIC HOLLOWNESS

In the hollowness of fanatic thoughts
there were no gods, no humanity,
no peace, but monsters.

The playful twins were lured
offering sweets and toys
and were sewn together back to back -
Onkel Mengele's holocaust experiments
of packing the tortured souls together to hell!

God, where were You?

In the hollowness of fanatic thoughts
there are no gods, no humanity,
no peace, but terrorists.

The holocaust continues
on myths, on hallucinations,
abstract, non-pragmatic ideology….

God, where are You?

FALSE EYE

All smiles are not alike,
yet, they're smiles, all like,
but the face, that is mysterious,
wears the mask of diplomacy.
However pure and innocent is love,
the world goes the other way round,
behind the mask hides the reality.
In the nook of human's mind,
truth, lies in fetters of falsehood,
that all are but just humans!
Yet human in the run for supremacy,
wearing the cloak of selfishness,
ascends the throne of self-made realms,
and smiles -
a smile of victory over his own clan!
False? Or true? Knows not unwary mind,
but a false eye will never see the truth.

FIRST DROPS OF NATURE'S LOVE

Dark clouds travel on the winds,
toward mountains, behind dry fields,
plants bow before mighty wind,
dust fills the air, shielding the sun behind,
sky hides behind the clouds,
whole village merrily dances
to welcome the season's first shower
of the nectar the nature's favour.
Clouds kiss the mountain heads,
so tender are their hearts,
in the mountain's mighty arms,
melt away, in love, the clouds.
The first drops of pouring love,
fill the earth's heart with love,
arouses the scent of wet soil,
and peasants get ready to toil.
The seeds wake up from their long sleep,
eager to break their shells and leap
into the fresh world of foliage,
to double the beauty of the village!

FROM SOMEONE WHO PERCEIVES THROUGH FLY EYES

Closing your eyes does not mean that you sleep,
wide opened eyes do not mean that they see,
but fly eyes with thousand lenses do
see the world hundred times a second.

You invaded my unconscious mind under
cover of darkness as I kept it always
as open as the sky. In a forest
I can find and name all wild animals,
but in this wily world who's who, who knows?
Behind the dark clouds, the rainbow is forced
to hide; and in a gutter I am coerced
to see colours - closing my mind, wearing
a fly-eye-spectacles, through bubble-wrapped
lenses, in a kaleidoscopic world
of imagery, which flies on the wings of time
on its own free will, in all directions.

Like the speeding lights of traffic on road,
nothing is visible to your glassy eyes
except reflections of light which arouse
no feeling. Exceptions are only to
prove the rule, they all have a mind of their
own, fully dreaming about what only exists
but in their imaginary world;
freak out to invade a fly's territory!?!

44

What is the use of your crystal eyes
when every bit of vision is perceived
through my fly eyes? I have a mind to lend
a few lenses; have a good vision.

GHANDI SPIDER SPEAKS TO ME

Intangibles too extend human moments
but not dreadful fantasies
of endless spitting and spinning
by a harmless herbivorous spider like me
whom you used unscrupulously
in the void of your imagination
to weave a biggest web of greatest designs
even a Goliath Tarantula can't
and in the end found a place
in your own world of records!

You know, me and my family
set out hunting for plants
to feed us and lead a simple life;
settled down here in this acacia tree,
dining on Beltian bodies and nectar
....

Oh! There comes a battalion of ants
we have no other way but to spit,
trail the safety lines of silk behind
to another peaceful branch below.

46

A GIFT FOR YOU

The presents of mind -
enrichment of relationships,
everyone likes to receive
and it is also nice to give.
The mind goes crazy,
going blank, running around shops,
looking for inspiration,
unable to give a shape
to the present of one's mind.
Here is a gift for you, you and you,
a gift of your wish and liking,
nicely wrapped and fastened
with golden ribbon,
bows of imagination atop!
How impatient are you,
you tear it open
to see the beauty
or to feel the fragrance of my love?
If you like it, my love is honoured -
the present of your mind for me.

GREED OR LOVE

Love and life are put to test,
anywhere, any time.
In the toilet
the gold ring of her love
slipped through his hand
and fell in the filth
he produced from his eats.
Unable to retrieve the ring
nor to flush the filth out
his feelings were crushed
between her love and the ring.
Who won?
His greed or her love?
Nobody knows, but himself and the ring.

IN SEARCH OF...

I knocked at the door of earth
with an empty mind, yearning for love.
Then I knocked at the door of man
to enjoy the brimming cup of real love.
As I grew, my knuckles turned thick-skinned,
knocking at the door of man for love.
Only resonance of silence
heard from behind the door,
provoking me to knock again and again.
Never to be knuckled under,
I continued knocking.
But the man behind the door was wily,
the last I raised my hands to knock at,
the entrance stood there without the door!
A flood of darkness greeted me,
as I looked in for a ray of love,
a canoe was floating in the darkness,
tempting me to row toward the light of love.
As I sat, with paddle in my hands,
I felt fountains of darkness splashing all over me.
Trying to plug the holes of canoe,
I forgot my mission; and I am still busy,
plugging the holes, in the darkness.

I Swear....

I swear, I've the power
to immerse the whole universe
into darkness,
even as the sun shines,
closing my eyes.

I swear, I've no power,
to light the whole universe
but to wait patiently,
till the sunrise

.

I swear, yet I have the power,
to light your face
with a smile, that'd sing
a thousand blended notes
of your pure and simple love.

I tread toward you, to be nestled
and feel the warmth of love forever!

I WAS THERE WITH YOU...

Yesterday I was there, just in front of you,
when you were busy, facing the computer,
your fingers working on the keyboard,
giving shape to your thoughts on the monitor.
I could see, through the window on your right,
the Christmas tree ornamented with candlelight,
right under the star of Bethlehem, when I thought,
I must not break the flow of your thought,
and I left just wishing you all the best,
but I doubt, whether you heard my voice.
Oh no! Don't cover your face with disbelief,
turn your eyes into your mind and tell me,
when you saw my greetings on the screen,
didn't you see me in your mind?

THE LEFTOVERS…

Serving in the wayside restaurant,
unlike vassals held fief and toiled,
holding on to my life I moiled,
cleaning tables, throwing away leftovers
among the greedy dogs behind the fence.
For a while, setting my eyes
on the fighting dogs, I would weep
thinking about my supper of leftovers.
And always tears
before sleep embraced the night,
eyeing the umbrella with a thousand holes,
light struggling for a passage to earth,
I would lay on the charpoy,
knocked out by tiredness.

Looking back now I smile,
as I cross my fiftieth year,
drubbed past writhes in pain
under the comforts of my future.

LIFE AND PEACE

Exasperated inspiration,
spirited arguments,
at last, extinguished fire,
buttered words of truce,
ashes of blind moments.
In isolation an exhausted mind
in self-imprisonment grumbles:
"Why all this fuss?"
Blatant confession of latent peace!

Peace slumbers -
in the vacuum between hate and love,
where sacred writings gather dust,
where no desires dare to enter;
there is no confession,
there is no fire of fury,
there is no religion, cast or creed,
there is no brokers of God....
Will there be a life?

LIFE OF HOPE

Life is a day, a page;
Every morrow, an unwritten page;
I turn a page a day of my life,
Only to see hopes striving for life.
Like the leaves of a tree,
Pages drop on my mind's floor,
decay, and on the rot,
Fall fresh ones, with dead hope.
The next page of my life,
I'm unable to leaf through,
for it hides behind
a camouflage of new hopes.
I browsed through the rotten pages,
nothing could I see,
except remains of dead hopes,
immoral children of unending desires!
Yet in the wilderness of solitude,
I see a flicker of light,
at the fag end of everyday,
of a living hope of tomorrow.
Eager to turn the next leaf of morrow -
Morrow, the harbinger of hopes,
I wish myself sweet dreams,
every night ere I go to sleep.

LIFE'S PATH

Life's path
is full of suspense and hidden traps,
without thunder, lightning spears.

On this Good Friday,
a life was caught unaware,
hit by a speeding truck,
leaving behind the mangled body -
a portrayal of amorphous life.
He was my friend's only future,
nurtured for nineteen years.

My friend now lives in the past,
for him, future will never resurrect.

LIFE'S ROADS

Released into freedom
of unfinished pathways
crossroads of doubts
asked for decisions.

A space of ambition
set me in temptation
to build my life
out of coloured dreams.

But all beautiful images
always show dead-end,
unless toiled with spade
into daily reality.

Dark ways left behind,
forgotten pathetic stories,
trial and error - turning points
to a new start to go on.

Behind the barrier ahead,
future brightens its head,
inspiring me to spade
digging into myself.

No road to freedom,
unless walking the talk,
realising that all roads
will make us free within.

LIFE'S STRING

Fighting death, falling in the graves,
leaving behind a legacy to follow suit,
life strides its contrived path and craves
for the eternal flame to live as a mute
witness through generations, looking for
gaps of momentary pleasures to forget
the morbid thoughts, and waiting for
another moment of glistening delight.
On the same wick the eternal flame lives,
through generations of perpetual desires.
If it is not for the selfishness that thrives,
why do we ignore the suffering of truth?
Are we not the same beads of the same string
of life of those struggling for a living?

MY FREEDOM

When I was set free,
I hurt you, my mother,
yet you greeted me with delight,
with a joyous smile on your lips.
The small pit on my belly,
is the memento of my freedom,
from a kindred dependence,
to the world of liberty.
Like the birds in the aviary,
within the man-made boundaries,
I saw the freedom,
struggling for liberty.
Ensnared in the crowd of restraints,
of customs, of colour, of creed,
suffering the agony in silence,
freedom struggled for liberty.
I pulled myself into a shell,
where my freedom lives,
with the boundless treasure,
of endless thoughts.
Back in the confinement,
of my pregnant mind,
I live now in the company,
of eternal freedom of thoughts.

MY LOVE

MY thoughts came to me
to pick up a sharp ray of colour to care
and to rule my forward path.
Under the umbrella of those tree boughs,
I found her as alone as me.
I said,
"Love me, as you love your life".
She graced me
with a smile and shied away,
to return to me forever.

MY NOTION

My notion -
echoed in green leaves,
as the wind blew
the leaves shivered even in summer,
and asked: "How warm is this life?"
A pale, off-white, colourless thought,
as nude as my cognitive content.

Life -
fills its pipe with time,
puffs clouds of smoke out
and asks to walk forward!

Green leaves -
you do not walk your life,
firm on your stalk
till to be detached from it
by the same wind you enjoyed,
to compose your future with the earth.
Learning lessons from you,
my future will have delight in wisdom;
newer buds, newer leaves,
but the same old wisdom.

MY SESTINA

Years went by, yet didn't die my desire,
O, Sestina, where're you, my poetic love?
Like leaves in autumn, days dropped from the stalk
of time,
but not my desire, from the stem of my mind.
To possess you, Sestina, my poetic beauty,
I've been wandering in the kingdom of words.

Waged a war, with the kingdom of words
To liberate you and quench my desire.
Wandered amongst the serenity of nature's beauty,
whilst writhed my mind in pain, longing for your
love.
O, Sestina, come out from your hide out and soothe
my mind
and let me feel the pleasure of a lifetime.

Life's so short and won't wait for time,
my mind's filled with fear, languishing for words.
I cursed the despondency of my mind.
O, Sestina, will I be able to fulfil my desire?
How can I dissipate the passion for your love?
When can I delight in your poetic beauty?

Spring came to embellish nature's beauty,
sprang up my mind with springtime,
flowers everywhere, spreading the aroma of love,
how'd I explain your beauty, I've no words.

Among the fresh foliage, peeped in my desire,
looking for Sestina, with a curious mind.

A supernova of hope woke up my mind,
and in the light I saw a glimpse of beauty,
Was it you, Sestina, my dream of desire?
A twinkle of hope, I saw for the first time,
my tongue went limp, unable to utter words,
whilst my eyes glowed with a fire of love.

My heart and soul choked with love,
as my thoughts laughed at my frenzied mind.
Blushed with shame, my mind uttered these words:
"How sad! I wandered looking for the beauty,
while she was within me all the time.
But I'm so happy, with my fulfilled desire.

O Sestina, my love, at last I found you, my beauty
With a jubilant mind, we'll now spend our time
Accept my garland of words and let me quench my
desire

MY VISION

Mind seeks the way of perception
from within the cage of boundaries,
tries to fit in the couture of cultures
and speak the language of mankind;
to reach unknown destination -
a world of boundless freedom,
where everything is only yours.

NATURAL COLOURS

Nature's green spread over,
on the bank of river,
nice bed for a siesta,
enveloped in coolness
of frolic summer breeze,
under shade of trees.
Kingfishers sit in bushes,
white ducks are ashore,
birds rest in the trees,
water hums to the tune of flow,
a song on solitary silence,
accompanied by a woodpecker's tapping.
Leaves rustle as breeze blows,
yellow leaves fall from foliage.
A chameleon in green, mingles with leaves,
dry brown leaves compete with breeze,
sky shows its nudity in blue,
drowsy eyes close their lids,
paving way for a dreamy darkness,
under the shiny afternoon sun.

NATURE

trees on the bank and
the hill behind, undulate
nature's mirror

hill in nudity
lush green pasture at its feet
nature's vestures

NON-EXISTENCE

The man searched his pocket,
his hands came out empty.
Walk, he was told,
to save on money,
for a penny saved is a penny earned.
He walked and saved money.

He searched his pocket,
his hands came out empty.
Run, he was told,
to save on time,
for time is money.
He ran and saved time.

He searched his pocket,
his hands came out empty.
Poor man still runs
out of money and for money.

OLD AND NEW

The same old roses, dahlias...
threw them all out,
planted new ones in place.
Newer sprouts, newer branches,
and on the day they blossomed,
I saw them spanking new,
but the same old roses, dahlias...
Nature's adamancy,
is your name old or new?

PAIN AND THE PAINFUL

It is not a pain -
a kind of torturing sensation.
head spins,
slowly a curtain of darkness falls,
vision faints, belly caves in,
sticky tongue licks the dry lips,
craving dies down.
On the anesthetic plain,
the emaciated body falls
with unknown but familiar uneasiness,
on the earth of human.
In a trance of senselessness,
the whole world disappears.
Death hides behind the pain -
the hunger, twin brother of poverty.
It is painful.
Neglecting the throes -
The struggle between life and death,
world thrives on sensual pleasures.
Forgets itself for a while
releases into this wily world
yet another life to suffer.
Life, ridiculously you failed
to learn from your past
and teach yourself the present.

PASSING TIME

The desert hugs sand dunes
in gorgeous curves of sand.
Rows of swaying palm trees
border the arid hill behind.

Gentle waves, bounty of the sea,
ripples glitter in the evening sun,
crabs scuffle eerily along the sand,
wheatears flick through the desert.

Coarse scrub along the dunes,
behind the horizon the sun dips,
a screaming flock of gulls flaps
lazily homewards up the coast.

Calmness descends along with darkness,
then fresh breeze blows in from the sea,
now in the growing peace of night
sleep embraces the lonely beach.
Hours of pleasure in nature's luxury
devoured by time. Passing seconds!
Fleetingly, stubborn time has gone,
I remain in the middle of glorious fall.

REAL SENSATION

Thoughts,
one after another, like waves,
hit the walls with force -
quaking the mind,
shaking the images,
blurring the vision.
Break the walls,
be open, like the sky above
to receive sensations of pain,
not the experiences of suffering.
Hold,
a thought, a sensation -
Sight, sound, smell, taste,
a touch….
That sends vibes to the soul.
Be that You,
my life's real sensation.

SAWING LOGS

Following the footsteps of his breath
snoring travelled into my ears,
hammering my eardrums.
His head was hitting
my shoulder at intervals.
When two dames entered,
sat behind and started:
"Chitter chatter, chitter chatter.."
The stertor came to a halt,
I released a sigh of relief.
Two stops later they got down
and the egghead grumbled:
"Calm after a heavy downpour"
and restarted his sawmill,
sawing logs till the end.

SEAT OF GOD

WHERE was the fane, when human was earth-
bound?
Where was the God, when there was no fane?
Who was me, when I was not conceived?
And was it me, when I came out of the womb?
Where is faith in my mind, when it is jailed in the
fane,
captive in the cell of beliefs, like valuables in vault?
Man, I salute your heavenly wisdom,
you protect in the divinely sanctum!
"He is in all and everywhere", you whine,
While, alas, keep on guarding the fane.
Where is your wisdom of faith, man,
when you protect Him who is saviour of all?
Weak is your mind, man, not the will of God,
else, why you immure Him in the man-made fane?
The struggle of distress is the outcome of faithless
faith,
in the hush of peace and not among the ruins of faith,
I see love in humanity, the strength that strengthens
my mind,
where lives my God, the saviour of mankind!

Separation

Sun embellishes the dewdrop
hanging from a leaf's tip.

This golden dewdrop
acts out a tale of detachment,

in silence.

SHADES IN SHADOW

"How many doors does your mind have?"
A question that he would weave,
posing with a smile, and would
invite me into his thoughtful world.
"Hey, please stop counting, my friend,
doors are narrow passages of mind,
break them all and the wall around,
let it be as roomy as this universe
it can contain the entire cosmos!"
The entire universe is now within me,
to sing on a holy world of future,
but I miss him a lot and his thoughts,
since the day I became penniless,
a state of status that detaches
me from the worldly relations.
I am not aware, why this happens -
in the dismal shades of logics,
the tree of life looks for shadows!

SLEEPLESS

Sleepless nights, artless thoughts,
the mind looks for lost links.
A sense of senselessness
as I scribble these lines;
syllables of poetic chaos,
spasms of sarcastic spells.
Setting trends, revising stands,
innovators act as modern Picassos.
Changing outlook stamps
oldies as obsolete rhymesters,
yet adorns the bookshelves –
a relationship with past glories,
relating the same old stories –
old loses its golden gloss.
Nonetheless, the past provokes,
the present seldom evokes.
A butt of rebuttal, extreme surliness,
soaked in deepest concoction
of old and new invention!

SO IS LIFE

In the desert
in search of shade
I wandered
and I found
my shadow.

In search of refuge
in my shadow
I tried to merge
and I found
no shade.

Had you been with me,
I'd have found
shade in yours,
and you
in my shadow.

THE SPIDER AND ME

The spider sat motionless,
spreading its legs,
capturing all the eight directions,
expecting the next prey for survival.
The writing pad and the pen
were idling on the table.
While my eyes were on the spider,
mind was spreading its tentacles,
in all directions, in search of a clue
to conceive an idea to fill in
the blankness of the white paper.
Mind followed drowsy eyes,
I switched off the lights,
Wishing myself sweet dreams.

STANDING OUT

I mingled with the crowd,
but no one noticed.
I stood away from the crowd,
but no one noticed.
I stood dressed in brilliant colours,
and they noticed!

Not me, but my dress.

STARS AND HUMAN

Of millions in the sky,
a few hold reigns of fate,
unfortunate are the unknown,
yet all are stars.

Of millions under the sky,
a few are fortunate,
unfortunate in the no man's land,
between boundaries of love and hate,
yet all are human.

STEALING A SHOW

Father denied money
to buy a ticket,
went around the tent
found an aperture
and concrete slab to stand on.
Like a cameraman of those days
focused on the stage
with one eye
stole the whole drama.

STRANDED

The day horizon of my knowledge expanded,
I commenced my lonely stride,
unaware where the path goes.
Sometimes I feel stranded;
anxious and exploding moments,
but the splinters will not hurt many,
for many are there like mine,
mines of minds floating in the ocean of life,
ready to blast at any moment,
so delicate, so dangerous;
afraid of the darkness ahead
the mind recoils,
the question mark looms in,
where to go from here, there is no lead.

SURVIVAL...

In the garden of thoughts,
I came across a grasshopper,
nature's tiny little creature,
hopping in pursuit of survival.

Why does it live, a life of mere existence?
Why does it survive? Because it is a reality?

On the day of its life's finale,
with nobody to mourn its death,
with no memorials, no prayers,
the poor soul would rest in peace.

From the boiling pot of emotion,
originated a steam of passion,
cooled by an air of imagination,
crystallized drops of glassy thoughts,
just to wither away in the heat of pathos.

Between the two extremes,
the fibril of life stretches,
throughout the length I hop
from one place to another
in pursuit of survival.

TALKING TO MYSELF

Like an irreversible force
meeting an immovable object,
I gather strength talking to myself
to push aside disappointments,
which taught tough lessons of life.
Now I venture to train my mind
to forget the past and look forward.

"Mind, stop your nomadic tendencies,
spice up your existence.
Listen to the dreams;
they make more sense.
stimulate your imaginations,
throw away the confusions,
tie up all the loose ends,
sit firmly in the driving seat,
steer ahead and let me feel
the winds of change."

THE FARMER

To thatch the dingy hut before monsoon,
to buy a bicycle for his son soon,
the father's dear-bought dreams were foiled,
the fifteen year old stands in the field.

Staring at dried sugarcane stalks,
his eyes emit vengeful sparks,
fearing what the future might yield
the fifteen year old stands in the field.

No takers and the crop perished,
his father's aspirations crushed,
and in the debt trap the life throttled.
The fifteen year old stands in the field.

Hanging from the old acacia tree,
his father at last set himself free,
'I'll blaze the crop', the boy yelled.
The fifteen year old stands in the field.

Economy grows, industries thrive,
everyone wants prices to nose dive;
farmers' ambitions die with no yield
the fifteen year old stands in the field.

Thousands of them committed suicide,
the heat of anger won't subside,
until the farmers' needs are fulfilled.
The fifteen year old stands in the field.

THE POET

A pen and a piece of paper,
the lost poet was re-created.
Sharpened his brain in serenity
to hear his mind's stupidity,
and was feeling the absurdity -
like a man, who had lost his legs,
yearning to scratch his itching toes.

"I would like to say
what I would like to say;
at distance donkeys bray,
what they would like to say?
This is a different way,
the feelings are wry,
the hay in the field is dry,
fire in the bush, and try
something will come out;
if not, please shout:
'you numbskull, shut up and sit out".

The poem was mere serendipity,
he was trying to be witty
with his head totally empty,
except for a feeling of mediocrity.

When his wife stormed in from kitchen,
with an oral list of pressing needs
rolling out of her swollen face:

"Find a job, man, and bring in something;
You and your rotten thoughts
………………………………"

Eureka! In the hollowness,
the truth of senselessness lies!

WAR AND PEACE

"The war is on",
The saviour of mankind declared,
"To bring in peace!"

"The war is on",
Yet another declared,
"To bring in peace!"

Killed many and sent to heavens
to mingle with
stars of martyrdom.
Fortunate are the departed,
Recipients of real peace!

"We've brought in peace!",
saviours of mankind declared,
"Those are great souls,
who sacrificed their lives,
may their noble souls
rest in peace!"

The living cried for the dead,
groaned for relief the wounded,
and the saviours rested,
whilst in peace
the departed rested!

WHO IS SHE ?

Alone, I stride into a coffee bar,
aroma of coffee suffuses the enclosures,
murmurs of customers mix with music;
crowd segmented around the tables,
sipping coffee, leafing through journals,
chattering and laughing away jokes,
gossiping on cellular phones;
roving eyes finding girls
poaching their privacy for piquant thrills.

Suddenly I see her in front of me,
dressed as a Snow Maiden, sparkly hat;
faint whispers, muffled weeping.
Before I reach her, she fades away.

I walk away with no idea who she is.

WORLD PEACE

Peace runs
helter-skelter,
seeking a piece of mind,
and finds a place among mindless
peaceniks.

YOU AND ME

Your words -
the mirror that reflects your face,
the strings of your voice,
the sweet intonations of love,
the free gift of God.

But I am sad He denied me,
the artistry to draw your face
clearer than your words
in the gallery of my mind.

Yet He was kind, let you
to be within me
though in my world of imagery.

FROM THE BEGINNING OF MY PAST...

ONE

In this world I have nothing to conceal,
so flows the shameless river like my life,
there are no stones to gather moss,
nor the golden sand of younger days,
only bed of civilisation,
where shadows of trees sleep coolly,
and sandy banks, now a grazing land.

The broken steps towards north,
reminiscence of a flowed down past,
leading to the old temple, where God
still lives in captivity, a dingy flame
struggling to confine the darkness.
How could He stay there, hundreds of years,
within four walls coloured by lampblack?

The gap in the centre of long green fence
is the entrance to my ancestral house,
surrounded by a variety of plants.
After sunset darkness reigned,
in those days of oil and wicks.
A huge elephant in black and white,
decorated the face of upstairs wall.

On the west, the road from the town
ends up unable to cross the river.
The river in the afternoon sun,
patches of shades and silvery sheen,

as I sit under tiled roof of main gate.
An irrigation trench passed through here,
a small waterway for children,
forgotten by time, merged with the road.
Paper boats now float in my thoughts,
contented life's intense joyful moments.

Path from the gate to the house
went with shoe flower plants
on both sides, till the courtyard
the heart of which a cemented floor
in the shadow of a group of trees
like a small carpet with a fading art
of design of kolam* touched the verandah

Entered the house - the center-stage,
where generations saw the light of life,
where my umbilical cord was cut,
where I spent summers of childhood,
with my grandma, the great manager.
Everything is old, but not memories
every time I visit, they grow stronger.
I began to wade through the fleshy
life's flashy ways, hugged by mother
as a month old babe, from place to place
like planets changing positions,
restlessly in twelve zodiac signs;
the flyway of life seems to be strange,
like paper airplanes of my childhood,
they never reached where I wanted.

So the wheels of life rolled towards south,
as the old train hauled the passengers,
hissing and whistling on the tracks,
spitting thick smoke and coal dust,
and I reached my father's house,
taken by my aunt, in my mother's words
into a dark corner of the thatched house
where lives struggled for existence and left
one by one leaving my father alone.

Morrows for him were non-existent,
yesterdays were stories to narrate.
He gave the present a flavour of taste
with his cookery and a smiling face
he was famous in his days
wherever he set up a way for our lives.
And he put up a coffee house
to feed us by feeding others.

Freed from oblivion of infancy,
memory gains its prominence,
empty brain begins to fill the vacancy,
like a scavenger, gathers moments
of pains and pleasures of retired past.

** Kolam is an auspicious art of decorating courtyards and houses, hand
drawn mainly by women and girls. Kolam is globally known as
Rangoli. Rice flour or sandstone powder is used to make rangolis.*

A toddler's luxurious days
are as bright as his hedonistic delights,
with a playful mind, an aimless life -
running between tables and chairs,
luring the minds of customers,
with infantile prattle and pranks -
an extra relish to their dishes,
I ruled the kingdom of innocence,
with abundant freedom of childhood,
where ends pure love's longevity
and begins a life of selfishness,
desire for the unnecessary,
a childish life's uncontrolled oddities.

Through the eyes of the wooden grill
I would catch the movements of rickshaws,
people walking their life of thrift,
cyclists peddling in haste,
vendors heading towards the beach
with head loads of merchandise,
the roads stretching straight on both sides,
alongside the parapet walls
guarding the canal that bisected the town
saving the park and the beach to the west.

Taxies were rare, but rickshaws -
transport of the social elite.
Clad in a lungi, a long towel
around his neck as a shawl,
or tightly tied around his head,
lifting the handgrip to his chest,

he would pull the carriage and run,
old sandals beating the road,
sounding the bell to clear the way,
a rhythmic sign of his presence in town.
After fifty years I saw him in Howrah -
a living beast of burden, but a man.

Shuttling between the town of canals
and my village, perhaps, I learnt
the route of nature's path of love,
in the warmth of sun and coolness
of a labyrinthine water world -
past resurrects, turns into present,
but the present is too different
from the resplendent world of past
untouched by humans of modern world.

As the boat moves, world travels back
jetty hides behind the dredgers
lake waits ahead with its mouth open.
Under the huge igloo of sky, the lake
adorns a green shawl around her neck,
the boat moves, alongside the bank,
fluttering ripples, wrinkles of lake,
stumble with bubbling noise - lake's whisperings,
nature's expressions; splinters of sun
scatter far and wide, silvery rays,
beaming out from undulations,
sometimes pierce through my eyes.
Shapeless creamy clouds move with wind
breeze brings in fragrance of lake water,

mauve hyacinths slither down the ripples,
drooping scrubs move up and down.
Ladies in lungi and blouse, beat
coconut fibre and wind the strands
on long spindles stretched in the background
of a row of their thatched dwellings.
Gliding down the calm and serene lake,
the boat swims between green clusters
of small islands - natures arabesque,
interlaced foliage in an intricate design.
At a distance, behind the dikes and bund,
an endless green carpet of paddy fields,
white herons changing their positions
appear and disappear magically.
The lamppost at the corner,
guiding light for the navigators,
changes the line of route,
alters the rhythm of pleasure,
from the expanse of lake to canal,
sound of engine ticks past slowly,
in the shade of coconut trees,
playful children wave their hands,
ladies wash crockery and clothes,
men repair nets for next day's haul,
flowers add colours to vegetation,
grazing cattle sharpen their ears,
noisy ducks float in the water,
a few yards away the jetty emerges.

The same route through night -
in nature's solitary isolation,

when she hides her beauty,
the boat would move like a firefly,
floating in the eerie darkness;
beam of light from the lampposts,
fiery eyes of the ghosts of night;
thickets and bushes, dens of monsters,
blinking kerosene lamp flames,
would peep out from the houses ashore,
sleepless stars would blink in fear,
and a frightened me would make,
the entire universe invisible,
curl up into a foetal position,
with my head in my father's lap,
in the feeble light of hurricane lamps
hanging inside from the roof.

*   *   *

My life's first five years in the town
ended with prolonged illness of my father,
in the pool of debt, the only refuge
was the village on the other bank -
transition from cosiness of a town
to an ordinary way of village life....

TWO

In this world I have nothing to conceal,
so stood the big pipal tree,
sprawling branches shielding the sky,
on an old square platform,
blanketed by green algae;
the paths from all directions
ended or began from here?

The heart of village gossips,
from Mussolini to Eisenhower to Mao,
local barber to bureaucrats,
the scene of discussions would hot up
under the influence of toddy
towards the end of every day.
Birds sang in chorus,
from their hide-outs in the pipal tree,
which followed the morning rays
and shadowed the path toward temple.
People from all the three directions
sincerely marched to the temple,
after an early morning immersion
in the river that encircled the village.

*   *   *

Sundays were auspicious for hair-cuts;
mother would pick up the harsh loud voice,
like coconut shell rubbing against rock,
and would alert me of the barber's

101

presence somewhere in the neighbourhood.

A lungi around his waist, a towel
on left shoulder, and an old
leather bag held under left arm;
an egg-shaped head, cropped hair,
staring eyes and a big nose,
a *beedi between thick black lips.

The leather bag - an antique piece,
inherited from his father years ago -
if it could, would have talked
the history of British India.
I was afraid of its contents -
scissors would not cut, but bite
the hair, like his old trimmer;
shaving knife would scrape the skin.
His garrulous mouth would produce
harsh sound and nasty smell,
choking up my ears and nose.

Yet sitting under a plantain tree
to undergo the ordeal -
a hard way of cutting down
luxuries of a barbershop.

The pond in the neighbourhood
just across the compound wall,
had enough water throughout year -
a swimming pool for children.

After the haircut straightaway
a dive into the pond from the wall
and hours together in water
would end up with mother's scolding.

A beedi is a thin, South Asian cigarette made of 0.2-0.3 grams of tobacco flake wrapped in a tendu (or temburini; Diospyros melonoxylon) leaf and secured with colored thread at both ends.

THREE

The archway to the temple of knowledge
opened up right in front of my small house,
green fences guarding the path,
thick growth, up above shaking hands.
Sometimes the path, intervened
by short-cuts between paddy fields.
My encounter with alphabets
commenced in the village school.
Sitting on the rough floor,
I drew the first letters,
with forefinger, in pink sand.
Then I was sent to public school,
In another village miles away,
the rightful choice for the poor.

My village -
with its verdurous vegetation,
fragmented by the river,
its branches and narrow inlets
piercing the land here and there,
an emerald gleaming in the sun,
neatly packed in lush green,
decorated with silver linings,
of the small water courses.
The inlets had palm tree logs
laid across, bridging the path.
Crossing the bridges en-route school,
miles away from my village,

barefoot, holding a dozen of books,
fastened together by a rubber band,
and a lunch box in one hand,
an acrobatic exercise of routine.
The path, created by footprints
of our forerunners, gave a look
of a brown carpet. Green grass
covered both sides, the mist
on them reflected the beams
of morning rays of the sun.
The growth of grass did not dare
to encroach the path, for fear
of destruction by human contact!
Alongside, the river flowed calmly
westward, yearning to merge
into vastness of lake, far away,
patting the broken banks;
herbaceous bushes drooping on her sides.

A rowboat or two passed by,
undulating calmly flowing water.
Trees and bushes reflected in the water,
produced a portrait of nature
against the background of cerulean sky
with snowy white patches here and there.
Except for the chirping of birds,
the children's prattles and the sounds
of falling auburn-tinted leaves,
calmness reigned all along.
A ferry and a hill intercepted
the path. Climbing down the slope,

105

between a pond at foot of the hill
and a field, led to the seat of knowledge.
Though not big, the hill raised its head
toward the sky, with its green crown.
Monsoon brought out fresh foliage
and doubled beauty of the crown.
Once in school, my mind used to yearn
for the blissful experience of returning home
in the evening, the same way,
enjoying brimming cup of nature's beauty.
Every creeper, searching supports;
every flower, unknown by name;
every sound of bird, falling leaves;
every image that reflected in the water;
all come alive in mind's screen,
at my wish. I learned to love you,
nature, from you. You taught me
the first lesson of natural love -
that blossoms in me everyday afresh
with flowers of innumerable hues,
dispersing an aura of fragrance!
Poverty is not a curse, but a boon,
a blessing in disguise, in many ways.
Outside my small, distressed world,
there was a world of blossoming nature.
I thank Him, who showered poverty
on my infancy. Or else I'd have walked a mile
to the next village, to be fetched by bus
to my school, leaving myself
deprived forever of my first lessons!

FOUR

Life grows eroding time,
leaves stumps of memories
like the fields after harvest -
short-cuts to my school.
With rains the muddy fields
compel me to take a longer path;
and an added burden of umbrella.

It is easy for a playful boy
to lose an umbrella,
deceived by a cloudless sky.
Rain takes me unawares
find a shelter under nearby trees
wait for the rain to reduce its force
and look for few taro leaves;
two of them to cover my books,
one for my head - an umbrella.

On the ridges many of them
in the cool breeze nod greenly,
raindrops fall on them, roll off in silver.
Dipping an entire leaf in water
I turn it into silvery green!

Back home fully soaked in rain
mother chews out angry words
I hear all with a smile
as she towels me with love.

A POEM IN A CAN

what gives this poem its misty fizz
is the opening hiss
emanating from the can

in insipid spaces between sips
burning calories of thoughts
mind hunts for meanings
in the blanks between blinks
between the words
lines and stanzas

nothing to latch on to
but this empty can of poem
and
a line of burp

A SOUVENIR

it is a canvass full of love
an unpolluted environment
that finds a home in nature's own colours
a priceless present

whenever her eyes fall on it
from any angle
her mind will paint

the day

ABSTRUSE OBTRUSIVENESS

sometimes poetry compels
words to bring in odd things
dyslexically daft lines
sans crucial words or a thought

penstock of words is open
on the paper they flow
until garishness is washed off
its lurid bad taste

then emerges a verse
as thin as a glowing filament
of an incandescent bulb
that I forgot to switch off
before sleep whispering through my nose
and it is still on in my head

ALIENATED PERCEPTION

it is still raining outside there

from the moving umbrellas
wetness slides down
unnoticed

relishing season's melodic percussion
I email the poem to many editors -
a poetic performance of building up
a world wide web of expert readership

a lone boy enjoys the rain
tripping the light fantastic
unnoticed

I close the windows
to keep the quietness within

AN AFTERNOON SHOW

nature bounces in a row of mounds
covered by mown lawn
the sun is cornered
somewhere in the west
behind the green strip

a leaf falls up
from a red rose flower
yellow and dry petals
fly up from the mango tree
pins of drizzling
explode bubbles
among undulations
a dog walks upside down
so also the people around me

drizzling stops
a little frog jumps from one
to another lotus leaf
an inverted catfish swims
to browse on algae

nature stands upside
down, fencing the sky below
churned into ripples

AN ABANDONED POEM

You too are ailing in the same boat

sorry there is a call from kitchen
water does not flow out of the sink
and I missed 's' in the first ailing line

You too are sailing in the same oat

sorry there's a call again at eight
in the morning, it's time to bring milk
and missed a 'b' before 'oat' in line five

You too are sailing in the same boat
like my wife and I, in the same sea
together without any complaint,
smoothly, despite rhythmic ups and downs
now this poem is an abandoned boat

BEHIND THE SURREAL WALL

You can see the wall from there, and hear
the mahout speaking to the elephant;
but what he says is not so clear.
Doesn't matter; but I am triumphant,

I could bring you closer to a scene.
I will ask you a question in the end,
indeed, it'll be about what you've seen.
Rest assured I will make no amends.

Allow your mind to follow what it says,
relying on your own thoughts and views;
they are all inventions in many ways.
I would be happy if my thoughts could amuse

you, and tell me now without fail:
the elephant was female, or a male?

BIFOCAL VIEW

the new year is sixty years old
directs my vision through a new pair
to regain the vision of my younger years

the ad tagged to the tail of the email tells:
"wow sixty year old now looks thirty
stunning result of a wrinkle trick"

and outside the window I see
a wrinkle-free morning

Clichéd tedium

vision hits the mist and returns
empty-handed in broad daylight
the day is no more darkly curious
stands on the edge of the world
where gods are left to take comfort
illusions dance on the vacant beach
beyond which water plays foam-and-run
distributes sparkling observations along the shore
reels of waves turn again
again
and again
to play the story again

A CURTAIN-RAISER

When the sun is about to set
she brooms - cleaning the dusty
residues of the day; the breath
of a violin stumbles and crawls,
sketching a tune of so subtle
a taste, swerves into my left
or right ear; may be branched out
of the music hall or a TV -
a suffered observation,
as my eyes fish through the window,
thoughts climb oranges of horizon,
and noise of mixer, grinder
makes the atmosphere roar.
I switch on the fluorescent light
which starts buzzing, as her devout
vocal music adds extra sound
accompanied by clattering,
tinkling and dripping from kitchen -
a timed musical opera.

DARKNESS AT THE END OF THE TUNNEL

wow! what a moving piece of work -
a nimble tread of a poem that walks

an array of words flows out
in a rhyme hitherto unheard of

powerful darkness stops the light
at either of the cliched ends

wagon loads of deafening sounds
pass by crushing my benign thoughts

and I walk alone towards light
having lost my work
somewhere in the darkness behind

DRIED VISION

ocean hangs
on the wall of horizon
day dunks
I stop when mind starts to walk
like waves
rush to the shore
vanish
drenched salty shore
long stretch of bare mind

EDITOR'S CHOICE

time hides under the eyelids
escapes at every blink
the way the soul looks the world -
a short flash of inspiration
like an ant discovers ocean
in a glass of water

a soulless vision in abstract of 1964
hangs on the wall: 'beauty dismantled'

thoughts swirl around the shapes
in the background of colourful patterns
a flowing river cutting through forest
or a blue herringbone design
under the sky of white clouds
hands hang down from naked waist
legs from shoulders
an eye on the left   a nose on right
bare breast at bottom
a horse-lion with its mane on wrong side...

there's nothing as embarrassing
as to confess one's ignorance:

"imagination and creativity are at their peak
but you should have sent us the painting
instead of this rotten poem"

LEGAL WAR AND ILLEGAL TERROR

guns are cheaper than poverty
a reality
costlier than the beliefs
as rooted embarrassingly
in stingy religions

more weapons are sold
than humanitarian aid to third world

more people are killed
than marijuana can
than suicide bombers can

white doves fly
olive branches in their beaks
bombs under their wings

FROM MY CAGE

So you are back home, and in the solitary
you will find yourself behind the bars of thoughts
about the monumental glories of past
about Delphi's temple, the inscription
that reads simple - 'Know Thyself', but contains
so many aspects of our lives. I am
glad, on the way you crossed our peninsula,
gliding through clouds under the blue sky.
Am I unfortunate, I do not know,
but feel fortunate enough to see the world
through you. For me my wings are cut
by the scissors of my bad economy;
through the bars of my cage I see, you fly.

GENERICISED WAY OF LIFE

Strings are attached and wound
around the brand names and spun
so the words remain yo-yoed
in one's brain!

As the Windows opens,
I open the window to my right,
no wind blows in,
eyes google through the window,
cloudy sky, dawn is a little away,
HTTP error 403, access forbidden,
and in my mind it is 404 -
page not found.

In the in-box on the screen
I am welcomed: 'No new mail'.
I turn off the PC
when a sound comes out, somehow,
through the closed door of bathroom:

'Where is my head and shoulders?'

That paints an ugly picture
of a human sans head and shoulders -
a dandruff-plagued thought
that needs immediate shampooing.

I-AM-BI(A)SED?

'If he can, then why I cannot?' is
a poser that I will never miss,
whenever I chance upon a sonnet
or a debate on it. Then I will start
surfing on the Internet to find
centuries old forms, how they rhyme,
where is the twist, syllable counts.....
I'll then open a new page on the screen,
giving a warning to my wife to leave
me for a while alone to devote some time,
somehow to produce a fourteen-liner.
My fingers will then refuse to type,
with no idea flowing down from my brain.
I realise finally it's not my job.

HOMEWARD COMMUTER

sandwiched between half-naked moon above my
head
and half-drown sun at the fag end of the street
the day is slowly forced to forget the world for
another night
inside me solid thoughts wait for words
as I walk in one of the galis*,
veins of bombay where commoners flow
where he knows me
I know him and his tea-shop -
an old table by wayside that carries
his entire establishment on its plane
and under it a warehouse of his daily needs

he throws crushed basil leaves, ginger and cardamom
into the saucepan of tea on the noisy kerosene stove
as the foam of reddish brown brew raises to the top
kills the flame and filters all the solid out

a cheering cup of tea of a few sips
the spicy sweet steam embalms my thoughts
and I'm ready to join the flowing crowd
to jostle my way into the crowded train
where there is no space for thoughts
every thought is about finding some leg-space

*galis means lanes

IDEAL READING

poet walks reading the river

suddenly he sits
on the edge of the bank
baits up the hook
throws the line
feeling the struggle pulls up

a big catch - a flawed reader

IMPRESSIONISM

I try to bring alive a scene
of our walking together,
his left palm in my right one,
to cross the road under the bright sun.

Except for a world of no hues
with impasto of noises,
he fails to define his feelings,
and leaves me in darkness.

KAFKAESQUE DEPARTURE

The note lying on the table reads -

In a world where ladder needs no rungs
staircase needs no steps, every step
is a belief, we believe, our life
is ours, only ours. we have the right
to use it and to dispose it of.

Travelled and lived in many countries,
made more money than thought of and spent
every penny on things that could
bring happiness and satisfaction,
leaving behind no debts or liabilities,
but money enough for our funeral
in the envelope there on the table -
our launching pad to another world.

Having lived a full life we now dangle
on a piece of nylon rope with two nooses,
for us this world has nothing more to enjoy.

MA GRIFFITHS

Certain oddness in phrasing of life,
which makes this poem individual.

"Improve it", she said, "by removing
words duplicate; but the quaint of it
I like, particularly of note,
I find 'days dropped from the stalk of time'."

Time has been running out steadfastly,
since the day she doffed her hat to me,
till she found a resting place in peace.
But I could not turn my handicap
of English not being my mother tongue
into an advantage, except that
I am still residing in her words -
all of them are still original.

VERDUROUS ANTICIPATION

in the grotesque silence of rabid spirits
loneliness opens the store of thoughts

thoughts cannot be dunes of desert
leeward side is never read by the wind -
a great loss of steep imagination

like trees act as if they strike and the wind
flies and hits and the clouds pour
and into the lake nature's mirror returns

inspiration is still under the dried thoughts
waiting for the green patches to reveal themselves

VANITY OF BELIEFS

great great great great great great great great great
grandfather piddled here at this spot where
his son   sons son and great great grandsons
do the same   leave behind a halo
of holy stink   clipping one's nose here
is a great sin of disobedience
beseeching them to stop the nuisance
is infringement of divine right

behind godly veil   humanity
is butchered on altar of false pride

divine right

TOSSING AND TURNING

in the gap between our backs
there is a rack of memory
for the books of our past
which we read in solitary

face to face we look at each other
read the haggard lines
of writings on our faces

we are one
but one of us will be alone
one day towards the end
leaving behind a lot
in the gap between us
to read about one of us

RAMADAN IN SOMALIA

in his mother's arms the boy said ta-ta
to starvation now lays on the mud floor
his dead eyes blindfolded with a coloured cloth
ready to be buried alongside a crowd
of small mounds of clay where dead children lie

she keeps her son's death a secret so as
not to loose his portion of ration too
to enable feeding his twin sisters whose
scared eyes witness the life's ghastly drama
unaware of what is in store for them

(2011 famine period)

DESPERATELY VEXATIOUS

it seems
mood is his occupation
sadness veils his face
he lives to march
whimsical life's aimless parade

anger opens a page of venom -
price of tension
drifts in his thoughts
in smoke of suspicion
that decorates
the edge of ferocity
impulses dance at random

throws down the smoldering butt
steps on it
grinds it
twisting his foot
with all fury
and satisfied
he walks away

I am still waiting for my bus

ALLUSION

Brobdingnagian wall -
a great effort to conceal
invisibleness

HUNGER

mind full of a picture
a piece of bread sans butter
and glass of water

LIKE THIS POEM

Hours together she spends
before the mirror
in different poses and styles.
Perhaps, she may be yearning
to see a good posture -
at least once,
from one of the many angles

MY NAME IS MASKED

The power of sound is in its radiance
every ray of it reaches the omnipresent,
who is present in unknown destinations.

Every time I am called: "Krishna...",
the real one too hears -
an advantage in disguise.
My being very naughty,
chances are more that
my parents must have called
our family deity a thousand times a day.

What an idea! I salute their wisdom,
which would usually go wacky in my presence:
"Krishna, you idiot, only thing you do is playing;
playing, playing and playing the whole day.
Did you do your homework, you useless?"

CURSE OF GOD (ISHRANK 30:15)

Without a mask you will not be a human; and
in a mask of human you won't be recognised.
Through the tips of hair your youth will escape in
black;
whereupon mask of ageing will descend on your
head.
A phantom creation of black and white war will
break out.
A blacked out face with glaring eyes will stare at you
piercing through the wall of darkness –
an adumbration of penumbra –
dreadful layer of rough and scaly fear
will resuscitate, frozen voice will melt, accent of
empty lungs will become familiar to the air
of graveyard. With wrinkling skin and innards and
dangling flesh, mask of ageing in the swamp of
mysteries will suck for baffling life.

HE, ME AND A MATCHSTICK

He is a life-long bachelor,
lives in the age of baldness,
fenced off by black hair on three sides,
expression lines separate
his calm-filled, round, clean shaven face,
squinty eyes under thin black curves
and a pudgy nose right in the middle,
thin lips seem to have never stretched,
the teeth will make a guest appearance
only in presence of friends like me;
a cream, half-sleeved shirt tucked into
black trousers with no belt around;
a thin man of resounding thoughts,
which play hide and seek on his face,
where expressions are often balanced
between frivolity and seriousness.

Always with a book in one hand
and a hanky in the other,
like a priest without a cassock;
for whom faith and fetish simmer
in the same cup of atheism;
religion is with no belly button;
beliefs are with no halos;
a free spirit in the old-fashioned way.

139

Whatever may be his greatness
he too has a great weakness:
'See the burnt heap of my past life'
he says, staring at the ashtray,
as if it is a notable feat.
He has never entertained
a friendly advice to stop smoking.

"How do you know what's and what
isn't good for me?' and continues:
'The first two sticks fail to ignite ;
the third one works , so it's a good one;
should I put it back in the matchbox?"

I now don't care about such souls;
yet it is a pastime to listen
to little banters, which may have
more truth than in the books
and, perhaps, I may attain moksha
without obliterating myself;
then where is the need for a Buddha?

POETIC NIBLET

minimalist
nibbles
at
a
thought

a
word
a
line

and
writes
this
entire
poem

OBSCURE LIFE

"Don't love me as much as you love your life,
in either case we have to part our ways,
I do not want either of us to chase,
this worldly mixture of concord and strife,
Be it a joy ride till end of the life,
let a split second end the phase,
a delightful send-off with a smiling face,
and let the comforts of this life be rife"
Ailing man failed to discern the kernel
of truth that not all wishes are fulfilled,
underwent all the throes and passed away,
love for his life must have fought a grim battle,
nobody smiled, but their eyes were filled.
I don't know what he had taught, till this day.

POETRY OF LIFE

when day goes far away
night comes silently
to share the bed

in the shade of love
thoughts of world cease
she occupies the mind fully

bond of love sticks
exchanges feelings
in dumb and deaf words

to transform into words
the mind is tongue-tied
paper is deafened

ON A RAZOR'S EDGE

I am on tenterhooks
the obvious response
to my concerns is:
relax, it might never happen

I don't care
even if it does happen
I'd been there
where I am now

but if I choose to relax now
I am sure to allow an opportunity
to slip through my fingers

I'd been there too
where I am now

PONDER IN SLUMBER

silence responds
from the soiled bed

where in the stink
somebody's soul dwells
alongside the invisible wraiths
beneath the tombstones
forgotten by time

the gulmohar knows nothing
but never fails
to scatter its red in every spring
and cover the old tomb

in silence breeze sings
tongueless words
a soundless poem
of now unknown dead

ON THE FAR SIDE

mind prods comely inspiration
unzips a wound enters a world of pain
in deepness the devil's paladin
beats luminous teeth in the fire

fading flicker alters the beach
beyond the black bark of the trees
journey of water continues
and he loses his way

leaches cavort about
the edges of sadness
curls of huge waves carry
him to the calmness of white shore

a bell rings somewhere
the sound wanders aimlessly
riding an argonaut that floats in the air
of the coetaneous urban blight

PROSTHETIC LIFE

wooden-footed future gathers lampblack
from the wick of life
when shadows seek to hide light
she looks for synonyms of happiness
in the lexicon of life

words fail -
singing and dancing
since the days of fairy tales
they have lost their shine

in the clichéd darkness
begrimed by the forerunners
travels the same time-bridged path
overburdened by footprints
towards the same destiny
one-footed

my sister

REDOLENT THOUGHTS

polishing the dull side of life I try
to see brighter side in a cup of tea
steam of an old recipe of smell makes
the inhibitions run away like the
charm of fresh rains which is as old as me
but lingers on, not in words but in smell
like the scent of first bloom from the first plant
in my childhood's first garden in backyard
jackfruit-leaf-spoon, steamy congee and spicy
chutney or the idli-vada-sambar
on a banana leaf in my father's
cafe of yore, or fragrance of his hard-work -
amalgam of individual tastes
an olefactive genre of old poetry

(F)IRE OF WORDS

words wrapped in fire
set ablaze the paper

crumbled ashes of
thoughtless words
unscathed by flame
fly transparently
in my mind
and you read them

on my face

VERSIFIED LIFE (A SE[MI]STINA!)

Each of the lines ends with a word,
poet gathers them to arrange -
a rosette of the flower of life,

fully bloomed image of tricky life,
no notion to draw hopes in words,
weak petals nobody can arrange;

but umpteen times mind can arrange
the garden of thoughts throughout his life,
teaming with imagery of words.

Half, mid, or late-bloomed buds of words
filled with unknown plans to arrange
the thoughts of hope in petals of life.

The secret is the fragrance of life
hides within the flowering words.
poet waits eagerly to arrange

the words in tightly stretched lines of
life's extravagant enjambments.

SOUND REASONING

a metallic clunk with reverberation
abruptly brought a droning thought to its knees
before a blankness of silence enwrapped it
which steams in   bends its spine   thrusts words   one
by one
a long parade in lines   in the lazy
grey cells   a simple recipe of spicy words with
simulating conditions...
please do not chuckle
after leading you to the perch of surprise
wonder   where did the metallic sound come from
is it some odd force meeting an immovable
object at home

the day-shaped darkness outside
declares it is going to rain right away

THE EDITOR REGRETS...

I salute you   the Bard of Avon
centuries have been consumed by time
yet your poems carry the same old flavour
I revere you   and agree   old is gold
but we need the most modern today
to survive in a surrealistic
market of neologism   please have mercy
do not disturb me   for I have to
eke out a life in a world where even
punctuations are in short-supply and
rising input-costs won't allow me
to permit the grand old inventions
I'm sorry   better try with someone
who lives in your era today

THROUGH THE FRAMES OF VISUAL ART

i walk, a load of sun on my head,
feeding on thoughts ideas go wilder -
sign of visual assumptions

spider weaves but not to cover
its nudity, candles carry flames
only to feed hungry darkness

branches of a dead tree draw
black lightening in the blue sky
not even a leaf moves in windstorm

tidal waves sweep my doorstep
the mountain of innovation
bathes in a tsunami of concepts

VISION

eye of the needle
is weaker
or
the thread has
lost its eyesight?

the camel is
still in a state of confusion

of the two
which is the right way
to the kingdom?

LIFE'S PUBLICATION

(1)
did I look at it
before I saw it
or
did I see it
before I looked at it

(2)
every blink pushes time
into the past
every moment is published

(3)
life walks
using the crutches of breathing
stepping into the past
after every step forward

(4)
life is the oldest book
without the pages
of beginnings and endings –
known unknown and/or published

THE APOCALYPSE

I was fortunate to know
someone who was unfortunate
or the other way round
but just one from many
a thin stint of friendship
like lightning drawing voice of thunder
breaking down the night for a split second

but familiar voices
of the nailed down unknown souls
from behind the thickening smoke
churned into black clouds
escaped from the twin towers
flapped across the East River
only to die down in nullity
of the world's largest graveyards of

Hiroshima
Nagazaki
Vietnam
Afghanistan
Iraq
Bosnia
Libya
Somalia
Syria........

destruction of the world

of the trapped
unknown humans
my friends
myself
me
awaiting
own destruction -
mutated eschatology of holocaust

stepping on humanity
grinding it
if you want to uphold
an unmerciful god
I will go for a godless world

let me throw away
this handkerchief drenched in grief
please give me another one

SNAPS

(1)

sense pauses
time passes
thoughts fight to end
the poetic menopause

(2)

dale lark sings around the bush
in vain for a world
when the words fail
my one-eyed friend
pixelates it all

(3)

empty can
cigarette butt
leftover of food
by the wayside
tell
there's no more time left in them

(4)

inside there's a story
ready to escape through this door
once the door is gone
the story vanishes

(5)

sun's snap of a tree
leaves mimic wind
in black and white
i stand on one of the branches
next to the bird
before focusing it flies away
with its snap

(6)

hospital bed
his limbs are numb
nose continues
to sniff life
that tries to walk
on the crutches
of weak breathing
perhaps few more steps....

(7)

dilapidated stone gate
one day it will fall
leaving the history
without an entrance

(8)

a paper at the news stand
cries out in bold
power-cuts are imminent

buckets and pots in queue
wait for the public tap to come alive

and the street light across the road
says it's darkness at noon

(9)

winter
wind blows
the tree has
no leaves
to tremble

Printed in Great Britain
by Amazon